# The Flawed U.S. Education System

By Elisabeth Heurtefeu

"If our education system had been imposed on us by a foreign country, we would declare it an act of war."
*A Nation at Risk (1983)*

# DEDICATION

I dedicate this book to the students I have known while being a teacher and a principal. I always held the belief that all children can achieve greatness if we just help them cultivate the curiosity they are born with, develop their skills, and find their bliss.

# COPYRIGHTS

Copyright © June 2017
by Elisabeth Heurtefeu

Paperback ISBN : 978-1-5215-0329-4
Imprint: Independently published

# ACKNOWLEDGEMENTS

To the friends, colleagues and parents who encouraged me to write this book, and particularly thank you to those who took the time to read it and give me their constructive feedback.

**Beverly,** you are the best principal coach I could have dreamt of and you were always supportive of my work and ideas.

**Denise**, you are true friend, attentive and supportive. Thanks for your sharp eyes spotting typos!

**Lielie**, thank you for your friendship, your contagious enthusiasm and encouragements!

**Suzanne**, you were a wonderful colleague during our years working as Chicago Public Schools principals.

# ABOUT THE AUTHOR

Elisabeth Heurtefeu is a dual citizen who has over thirty years of experience in the French and American education systems, as a student, educator and administrator.

In France, she graduated with degrees in business and education. In the USA, she received a Masters degree in Leadership Education from Northeastern University and a Masters degree in Math from DePaul University. She worked in the U.S. as elementary school teacher and director at the Lycée Français of Chicago (3-18 years old private school), then as principal at LaSalle Language Academy (a K-8 Chicago public magnet school offering four foreign languages in addition to the regular U.S. curricula).

At the end of her tenure, LaSalle Language Academy was recognized as a

2015 National Blue Ribbon school, the highest national award for excellence. Elisabeth Heurtefeu also received the "Palmes Académiques" from the French government for her role in promoting the French language and culture during her twenty-year career in the United States.

She felt that writing this short to-the-point book was a duty to share her experience and views on how to fix a deeply flawed U.S. education system.

# TABLE OF CONTENTS

**Introduction**

**Chapter 1**
**Education Is Not a Right**

**Chapter 2**
**The Absence of Universal Free Preschool**

**Chapter 3**
**The Funding System**

**Chapter 4**
**The Rise of Poverty**

**Chapter 5**
**The Testing Disaster**

**Chapter 6**
**Teachers**

Chapter 7
The Privatization of Public Education

Chapter 8
The Elementary & High Schools Curricula

Chapter 9
The Outrageous Cost of Higher Education

Chapter 10
Trapping Citizens for Life Via Student Debt

Chapter 11
Missing Out on Human and Economic Potential

Chapter 12
Steps towards Radical Change

# INTRODUCTION

There is a perception that the United States of America offer an exceptional education system. Unfortunately, this is not the case. This reputation is often based on the excellent ranking of a few U.S. universities in the world but the U.S. education system has many flaws.

The truth is that the very expensive elite U.S. universities attract the smartest and most renown professors from all over the world, often because they are offered much higher salaries than in their country of origin. However, despite this influx of intelligent brains at the University level, the systems put in place to educate American children from birth to 12th grade are a disaster.

I am using purposely strong words such as disaster and catastrophe to open the eyes of the American parents and encourage them to demand change. They are so used to what is in place that they have lost the capacity to research, compare, analyze, and revolt. As teacher and principal during my 20-year career in the U.S., I have met with hundreds of parents and I was shocked to see that very few were informed about the better education systems that exist in other developed countries. When speaking to the parents, I painted a picture of a better, less expensive, and more successful educational approach that is available in Europe and Asia.

The American parents I met at the Lycée Français of Chicago were somewhat better informed because they knew that having mastered the French curriculum in K-8 succeeded by the French Baccalaureate at the end of 12th grade would place their children in the most competitive position for college applications. But this came at a huge cost, with an average (in 2016) of $16,000 a year per child! From 3 through 18 years old, we are talking about 15 years at a total cost of $240,000. It is easy to deduct that only wealthy families can afford that investment for one child!

A society is richer when it ensures the development of its youth and helps them realize their full potential, not when it produces the most goods, which is still how countries are measured and compared. In March 2017, the United Nations Sustainable Development Solutions Network published its yearly *Happiness Report* prepared in collaboration with the Earth Institute at Columbia University. Norway received the rank #1 followed by Denmark, Iceland, Switzerland, Finland, Netherlands, Canada, New Zealand, Australia and Sweden. The United States ranked 14. What is one of the important reasons why the people in Norway are so much happier than the U.S.? While hundreds of thousands of bright, young Americans don't go to college because they cannot afford the cost, public college in Norway is tuition-free, allowing all citizens to pursue their career of choice.

The number of students affected by a less than adequate U.S. education system is around 50 million, approximately 15% of the United States population. In elementary school (Pre-K through 8th grade), there are 35.4 million while 15 million are in high school (grades 9 through 12). An additional 5.2 million students are attending private elementary and secondary schools, approximately 1.7 million are homeschooled and 1.3 million children are attending public pre-kindergarten. (source: U.S. Department of Education, September 2016).

After examining the most important flaws of the U.S. education system, I will offer possible steps towards a much needed and radical change.

# CHAPTER 1

# EDUCATION IS NOT A RIGHT

Constitutions usually establish powers, rules and duties and safeguard essential rights. Surprise! In "the most powerful country on Earth", the U.S. Constitution is silent regarding the right to education. Written to guarantee above all Freedom, not Equality, the right to vote, to bear arms, freedom of speech, religion, press and right to assembly were not forgotten. However, the Founding Fathers did not consider the right to education. At the time, it probably made sense: were they going to promise to educate children and take them away for six hours a day when their work was needed in the fields and in nascent factories?

To be fair however, while education may not be a "fundamental right" under the Constitution, the equal protection clause of the 14th Amendment requires that when a state establishes a public school system, no child living in that state may be denied access to schooling. One can wonder though why, in the 21st century, Congress still has not formally recognized education as a universal right? Every country that outperforms the U.S. in the academic performance of its youth has a constitutional or statutory commitment to the fundamental right to receive an education.

In the absence of this constitutional right, states have the freedom to decide if education should have a major place or not. Each state is also left with the complex task of designing its own educational systems.

Over the years, Acts were voted by Congress to regulate some aspects of education and support the states with federal grants substantial enough to encourage states to file requests. For instance, **the federal Elementary and Secondary Education Act (ESEA) passed in 1965 as part of the U.S. President Lyndon Johnson's "War on Poverty"** attached the following grants to the Act:

- Title I—Financial Assistance to Local Educational Agencies for the Education of Children of Low-Income Families (schools must have at least 40% students that qualify as low income)
- Title II—School Library Resources, Textbooks, and other Instructional Materials
- Title III—Supplementary Educational Centers and Services
- Title IV—Educational Research and Training
- Title V—Grants to Strengthen State Departments of Education
- Title VI—General Provisions

The Elementary and Secondary Education Act (ESEA) emphasized equal access to education and imposed standards for accountability. Note that **"equal access"** does not really guarantee equality of access. Having "equal access" to Harvard or Yale University does not mean you can afford to enroll your children at $50,000/year!

The ESEA first reauthorized by Congress every three years then every five years. Often, the Presidents gave the Act a new name to put their own "brand" on education. Under Reagan in 1981, it became the Education Consolidation and Improvement Act (ECIA). In 1994, under Bill Clinton, it was named Improving America's Schools Act (IASA). Later, with George W. Bush, in 2001, ESEA was known as "No Child Left Behind" (NCLB), a politically motivated "brand" to sell a lie and set impossible goals for schools, such as achieving 100% success in standardized tests. Under President Obama in 2015, the ESEA was reauthorized by Congress as the "Every Student Succeeds Act" (ESSA), another marketing name to sell a fancy wishful thinking name to the public.

Over the years, essential other grants were added to the Act in the form of amendments to take into account students with special needs.

**1966 amendments (Public Law 89-750) -** Title VI – Aid to Handicapped Children (1965 title VI becomes Title VII)

**1967 amendments (Public Law 90-247) -** Title VII – Bilingual Education Programs (1966 title VII becomes Title VIII)

Since 1776, the United States could have recognized Education as a fundamental constitutional right but it did not happen. There were many missed opportunities.

# Missed Opportunities to Make Education a Right

## Missed Opportunity #1
## The Second Bill of Rights

The Second Bill of Rights also called the "Economic Bill of Rights" was a list of rights proposed by President Franklin D. Roosevelt during his State of the Union Address on January 11, 1944. **Roosevelt's argument was that the rights guaranteed by the U.S. Constitution and the Bill of Rights had "proved inadequate to assure equality in the pursuit of happiness"**. He wanted to guarantee eight "economic" rights: employment, food, clothing, leisure, farmers' rights to a fair income, freedom from unfair competition and monopolies, housing, medical care, social security and education. In present times, he would be called with disdain a socialist! His proposals would have changed the USA in a social democracy, nothing "socialist" in the Marxist interpretation of socialism. Some parts of President Roosevelt's address below are very similar to the passionate discourse of 2016 democrat presidential candidate Bernie Sanders. Roosevelt was convinced that the new rights would guarantee American security and the U.S. place in the world. Unfortunately, the Congress never adopted these rights.

## FDR Speech to Congress (1/11/1944)

"It is our duty now to begin to lay the plans and determine the strategy for the winning of a lasting peace and the establishment of an American standard of living higher than ever before known. **We cannot be content, no matter how high that general standard of living may be, if some fraction of our people—whether it be one-third or one-fifth or one-tenth—is ill-fed, ill-clothed, ill-housed, and insecure.**

This Republic had its beginning, and grew to its present strength, under the protection of certain inalienable political rights—among them the right of free speech, free press, free worship, trial by jury, freedom from unreasonable searches and seizures. They were our rights to life and liberty.

As our nation has grown in size and stature, however—as our industrial economy expanded—**these political rights proved inadequate to assure us equality in the pursuit of happiness.**

We have come to a clear realization of the fact that **true individual freedom cannot exist without economic security and independence. "Necessitous men are not free men."** People who are hungry and out of a job are the stuff of which dictatorships are made.

In our day, these economic truths have become accepted as self-evident. We have accepted, so to speak, a second Bill of Rights under which a new basis of security and prosperity can be established for all—regardless of station, race, or creed.

Among these are:

- The right to a useful and remunerative job in the industries or shops or farms or mines of the nation;
- The right to earn enough to provide adequate food and clothing and recreation;
- The right of every farmer to raise and sell his products at a return which will give him and his family a decent living;
- The right of every businessman, large and small, to trade in an atmosphere of freedom from unfair competition and domination by monopolies at home or abroad;
- The right of every family to a decent home;
- The right to adequate medical care and the opportunity to achieve and enjoy good health;

- The right to adequate protection from the economic fears of old age, sickness, accident, and unemployment;
- The right to a good education.

All of these rights spell security. And after this war is won we must be prepared to move forward, in the implementation of these rights, to new goals of human happiness and well-being.

America's own rightful place in the world depends in large part upon how fully these and similar rights have been carried into practice for all our citizens. For unless there is security here at home there cannot be lasting peace in the world."


We see that President Roosevelt was addressing all the rights that Americans are still fighting for. If the U.S. Constitution do provide strong protections for civil and political rights, it still fails to recognize economic and social rights.

Sometimes, the right to education can be found in a few state constitutions; others, such as the right to an adequate standard of living including food, shelter, and medical care, are still not guaranteed.

As a result, economic, social, and cultural issues are not rights recognized for all, and public policies can exclude people from eligibility as long as they do not discriminate on grounds such as race or gender. It is a crucial issue in a country like the United States that is still the wealthiest in the world as measured by the GDP.

**Missed Opportunity #2**
**Amendments Regarding the Right to be Educated**

Of the over 11,000 proposed amendments to the Constitution thus far, only a couple have addressed the right to an education. Rep. Major Owens (D-NY) and Rep. Jesse Jackson Jr. (D-IL) introduced the same education amendment from 1999 to 2012 proposing "the right of all citizens of the United States to a public education of equal high quality." During these trial years, the maximum support only reached 37 Democrats cosponsors. The resolution was always "killed" in the House Judiciary Committee.

**Missed Opportunity #3**
**The International Covenant on Economic, Social and Cultural Rights (1966)**

The International Covenant on Economic, Social and Cultural Rights is part of the International Bill of Human Rights and is the only covenant that requires governments to promote and protect such rights as health, education, social protection, and an adequate standard of living for all people. The ICESCR has been ratified by more than 150 countries. President Carter signed the

Covenant in 1977, but it has yet to be ratified by the United States.

## Missed Opportunity #4
## The International Declaration of the Rights of the Child

The rights of the child were proclaimed by General Assembly Resolution on November 20th, 1959 and adopted by the UN General Assembly 30 years later on November 20th, 1989. The Convention on the Rights of the Child entered into force on September 2nd, 1990 and **was ratified by all countries except the U.S.** It was never sent to the Senate for approval. **In Principle 7, the International Declaration states that "the child is entitled to receive education, which shall be free and compulsory, at least in the elementary stages.** He shall be given an education which will promote his general culture and enable him, **on a basis of equal opportunity**, to develop his abilities, his individual judgement, his sense of moral and social responsibility, and to become a useful member of society."

We can guess that the Congress, (whose members are often elected with large contributions of powerful lobbies) never wanted to guarantee an education based on "equal opportunity". The American education system stays profoundly unequal because there is no desire at the top to shift vast amounts of funding from the defense budget to the education budget.

## Is Education at Least a Right at the State Level?

Unfortunately, education is rarely recognized as a right. For instance, in Illinois, education is described in Article X of the Constitution of the State of Illinois as a goal, not a right.

## Illinois Constitution, Article X, Section 1

"A fundamental goal of the People of the State is the educational development of all persons to the limits of their capacities. The State shall provide for an efficient system of high quality public educational institutions and services. Education in public schools through the secondary level shall be free. There may be such other free education as the General Assembly provides by law. The State has the primary responsibility for financing the system of public education." (Source : Illinois Constitution.)

In the Illinois Constitution, there is no free public school provision for preschool and for university education; no word either on vocational and non-traditional students. The state has the responsibility to finance the system of public education but the Constitution does not define the range of responsibility nor state percentage in the financial responsibility for education.

Once we know that education has never been recognized as a fundamental right in the U.S.A., we understand why, with an absence of basic commitment, education systems are flawed. How interesting in comparison that the right to bear arms was not forgotten!

# CHAPTER 2

# THE ABSENCE OF UNIVERSAL FREE PRESCHOOL

Almost everything conditioning and unleashing the power of the brain happens before six years old. This is well explained in the book *"How to Parent"* published in 1970 by the American psychologist Fitzhugh Dodson. In the French version, the book title was translated: "Everything happens before six years old" ("Tout se joue avant six ans.")

Unfortunately, most states do not provide free universal preschool at three years old. At Harvard Graduate School of Education, Ronald Ferguson, director of the Achievement Gap Initiative, studied every identifiable element contributing to unequal educational outcomes.

He particularly has been looking at improving children's earliest years, from infancy to age three because research indicates that a gap in language, gesturing, and other developmental markers begins to open as early as two years old.

During my career in education, I have seen tremendous differences between a child who has received a rigorous education before six years old and one who has not. This is not always due to socio-economic status differences. Some wealthy busy parents often leave their children with babysitters who rarely have received advanced degrees. For example, the number of words known and understood can vary
considerably whether or not a child has been exposed to some form of education at home or in preschools. In the U.S., very few public school districts offer pre-Kindergarten and the realization that this might be a mistake is not enough to fund more preschools.

As a result, in 2014, the percentages of 3 and 4-year-old children enrolled in various pre-primary* (including private) programs were 43 and 66 percent, respectively. The percentage of 5-year-olds enrolled in pre-primary programs declined from 89 percent in 1990 to 85 percent in 2014.

**SOURCE:** U.S. Department of Education, National Center for Education Statistics. (2015). *The Condition of Education 2015* (NCES 2015-144), Preprimary Enrollment.

*Note: "Pre-primary programs" are groups or classes that are organized to provide educational experiences for children and include kindergarten, preschool, and nursery school programs. Children are not going for a full-day but often a half-day and not for a full-week. "Educational experiences" do not compare to a rigorous curriculum.

Very often in the United States, only the children of middle and upper class parents have the opportunity to be enrolled in private preschools while other children stay at home, receiving no formal education. When both parents work, and do not have the means to pay a nanny, children are sometimes left with the grandparents or other relatives living nearby until they reach the age of Kindergarten.

In reality, few American parents can afford quality private preschools. Many children less than 5 years-old do not receive the stimulations that would help them achieve much more in their lifetime. Think about the waste of potential development for the children who did not go to school before Kindergarten!

Even for families who have the means, private preschools vary immensely in quality, from just day care to so-called Montessori using a famous educator's name from the early 20th century to pretend there is a serious curriculum. Private pre-schools are not bound to teach rigorous and adequate early childhood curricula.

In contrast, in France, free, full day public education starts at 2 and a half years old, resulting in four school years of formal education with a rigorous curriculum before the child reaches 1st grade. The attendance is extremely high: 98% for 3 year old and 99.9% of 4 and 5 year old.

Source: http://www.education.gouv.fr/cid57096/reperes-et-references-statistiques.html#Données_publiques

The French preschool programs are written by highly qualified educators at the Ministry of Education and offer a well thought-out national curriculum which is revised, if necessary, approximately every seven years. The French preschool is the number one equalizer of chances for all. Because it starts as early as two and 1/2 years old, it allows children from all backgrounds and socio-economic status, including those of immigrants, to master the French language and be given equal opportunities of success as a result.

# CHAPTER 3

# THE FUNDING SYSTEM

When I was studying for the Masters in Leadership Education in Chicago, Illinois, I could not believe how unfair education funding is in the United States. The university professors were somewhat resigned about the way things were and conveying that changes were not on the horizon. Unfortunately, they were right!

The two main sources of funding for school districts are the real estate tax at the local level and the supplemental funding at the state level. State level funding occurs if the revenue from the real estate tax does not reach the minimum level per student decided each year by the state legislators. A minimum portion of funding comes from the federal government. As an example, in Illinois, in 2014/15, the funding was split as follows:

Local:   $ 18 Billion   67%
State:   $ 6.7 Billion   25%
Federal: $ 2.1 Billion    8%

TOTAL:  $ 26.8 Billion

This system would somehow work if all states were setting the minimum per student at an adequate level. Unfortunately, many states have funding formulas that are not sufficient to create the conditions of quality education.

School districts located in wealthy neighborhoods rarely qualify for general state aid because they benefit from high property taxes. School districts located in impoverished neighborhoods receive supplemental funding to reach the minimum decided by legislators of the state.

Basing education funding on real estate taxes is by design creating inequality. In order to benefit from more resources for their children, American parents have to carefully consider where they decide to live. There are many stories of pregnant parents starting to worry about where to live based on a school district wealth. If parents can afford to live in an area where houses are expensive, their child will have better chances to succeed. In reality, only middle and upper class families can afford that choice. This funding system increases the gaps between rich and poor instead of closing them.

The inequality also varies greatly per state and per district regarding the dollar amount spent for expenditures per student. In 2013/2014, the U.S. average for public elementary and secondary schools was $11,355 per student.

States with the highest expenditures per student were:

| | |
|---|---|
| Vermont | $21,263 |
| New York | $20,428 |
| New Jersey | $20,117 |
| Alaska | $19,244 |
| Rhode Island | $18,627 |

The states with the lowest expenditures per student were:

| Arizona | $7,143 |
|---|---|
| Utah | $7,476 |
| Oklahoma | $7,925 |
| Indiana | $8,135 |
| North Carolina | $8,632 |

The difference is up to $10,000 spent per-year per-student between states! It is worth it for parents to consider a move to Vermont!

Source: http://www.nea.org/home/rankings-and-estimates-2014-2015.html

When it comes to contributions in percentage of education funding, Illinois ranks last, yes, 50 out of 50, contributing barely 20% for educating K-12 students compared to a national average of 45%. The trend is not encouraging for the future: Illinois spent 9% less on general state aid per student in 2015 than it did in 2010. The state of Illinois has earned an
"F" in funding distribution for 2007-2012, the latest year for which figures are available. Illinois hasn't even paid the minimum 2010 per-pupil funding (very low) level of $6,119!

Source: http://www.ilraiseyourhand.org/statefunding

The inequity between poor and rich districts is due to the high disparities in home values which are the base for the real estate tax. As a result, high-poverty districts spend much less on education than wealthy districts do. For example, the Winnetka District 36 spends $19,774 per student while high-poverty Bartonville District 66 spends $7,451 per student, an alarming difference of $12,323 per student. Shouldn't it be the opposite? High poverty districts should receive twice as much as wealthy districts to properly address the needs of their students and bridge the gaps that exist already before a child enrolls in Kindergarten.

According to Harvard Graduate School of Education Dean James E. Ryan, geography mirrors achievement levels because it determines educational opportunity in America. In his book "Five Miles Away, A World Apart" (2010) he shows the disparity of opportunity in two Virginia, schools, one located in a poor urban neighborhood and the other located in a wealthy suburban district. He concludes: "Our education system, traditionally thought of as the chief mechanism to address the opportunity gap, instead too often reflects and entrenches existing societal inequities."

Everybody knows about the inequity of education, even the Supreme Court, as shown in this opinion:

The United States Supreme Court declined the opportunity to intervene in San Antonio Independent School District v. Rodriguez, where the Texas school financing system was challenged because of the huge disparities that resulted between high-wealth and low-wealth districts. The Court characterized the Texas system as "chaotic and unjust" and emphasized the need for reform in a tax system that "relied too long and too heavily on the local property tax."

Source: "Fund-amental Disparities: Illinois Education Financing and the Need for Reform. Leslie Cornell http://www.luc.edu/media/lucedu/law/centers/childlaw/childed/pdfs/2012studentpapers/cornell.pdf

Historically, upward mobility in America was characterized by each generation becoming better educated than the previous one, said Harvard economist Lawrence Katz. But that trend is weakening, particularly for minorities. This sad reality is the consequence of a funding system that has been increasing the gaps between the poor and the wealthy.

# CHAPTER 4

# THE RISE OF POVERTY

A study conducted in 2013 by the National Student Clearinghouse Research Center, reveals that family socio economic status — not race, ethnicity, national origin or where you attend school — is the best predictor of college attendance and completion. High-poverty high schools sent at best half their class of 2012 graduates to college, compared with 70 percent of graduates from higher-income high schools.
Source:
http://www.edweek.org/ew/articles/2013/10/23/09college.h33.html

The reality is that the median income in the U.S. has decreased since 1999. In 2015, real median household income ($56,516) was 1.6 percent lower than in 2007, the year before the most recent recession, and 2.4 percent lower than the median household income peak that occurred in 1999.

In 2015, there were 43.1 million people in poverty, 3.5 million less than in 2014. However, the 2015 poverty rate was 1.0 percentage point higher than in 2007, the year before the most recent recession. According to the National Center for Children in Poverty, "about 15 million children in the United States – 21% of all children – live in families with incomes below the federal poverty threshold, a measurement that has been shown to underestimate the needs of families. Research shows that, on average, families need an income of about twice that level to cover basic expenses. Using this standard, 43% of children live in low-income families."

In Finland, the child poverty rate is about 5%, so no surprise that the Finns outpace the U.S. students.

Sources:
https://www.census.gov/library/publications/2016/demo/p60-256.html

http://www.nccp.org/topics/childpoverty.html

Researchers Michael Rebell and Jessica Wolff (Campaign for Educational Equity at Columbia University) even claim that there is no general education crisis in the United States but there is a child poverty crisis that is impacting education.

Low-income children fact sheets are available online at http://www.nccp.org/publications/fact_sheets.html and illustrate the severity of economic instability faced by low-income and poor children throughout the United States. A "poor household" is one where the total income is below the federal poverty threshold ($24,036 for a family of four with two children in 2015). Families with earnings less than twice the poverty threshold are considered low-income. According to NCCP researchers, the number of children in low-income families increased slightly from 42 percent in 2009 to 43 percent in 2015, and the percent of poor children in the U.S. increased by 1 percentage point.

Spending for education has not kept pace with the rise in child poverty. While poverty grew by 40% in the Midwest and 33% in the South from 2001 to 2011, educational spending per pupil grew by only 12% in these regions over the same 10-year period. Billions of dollars were spent in the U.S. on programs such as food stamps, welfare, Medicaid, and Head Start. Yet the root cause was not treated.

The hundreds of millions spent by Arne Duncan, President Obama's Secretary of Education would have been better used helping states build high performing preschools to educate children before Kindergarten. The world's most prosperous nation has yet to prioritize investments that benefit the majority of people, not the top one percent in order to avoid becoming the largest banana republic of the world.

# CHAPTER 5

# THE TESTING DISASTER

Coming from France where exams are mostly essays evaluated by certified educators (not by remote, for profit, testing companies), I had no idea that multiple choice tests were the main way to evaluate students in the U.S. The first time I took such a test myself was when I was told I needed to pass the GRE in order to be accepted in the Masters Leadership Education program. I found the GRE easy because there was no dissertation, no need to prove that I could discuss ideas, provide and defend good arguments, show that I could express clearly my thoughts, explain how I reached a conclusion in solving a lengthy math problem. I quickly realized that I should only review preparation books for a month and there should not be any problem. Other Europeans I met found these tests ridiculously easy.

After all, the answers are given among the different choices!

The GRE is an Educational Testing Service (ETS) test evaluating math and reading. In the United States tests are rarely conceived and graded by teachers; they are often created by retired educators hired by companies whose goal is first and foremost to preserve their market share and profits. They employ lobbyists in Washington DC and in the different state capitals to influence politicians. Contributions to the politicians' campaigns guarantee that their interests will be preserved when new legislation comes up for a vote.

Since George W. Bush's "No Child Left Behind" Act passed in 2002, the amount of student testing has skyrocketed. Under Bill Clinton's Improving America's Schools Act, students had to take six reading and math tests in elementary, middle and high school. Under NCLB, in order to qualify for federal funding, the government mandated that states implement 14 tests (reading and math tests from grades 3-8 and once in high school, plus a science test in elementary 4th grade, middle 7th grade and high school).

In 2009, Obama's Race to the Top did not slow down the pace of standardized testing. On the contrary, it required states to change their laws to increase accountability of teachers and school administrators via student testing. For example in Illinois, this resulted in even more standardized tests. Not only was ISAT (Illinois Standards Achievement Test) maintained once a year in mathematics and reading from 3rd through 8th grade but the State of Illinois also mandated that districts test children several times a year from Kindergarten through 12th grade to measure yearly growth of students and base the evaluation of teachers on these measures. Any parent knows that a child does not grow linearly. There might be a year where the child remains at the same height, and years where the child grows four inches. It is the same way with the brain. Basing the evaluation of teachers on a one-year growth in mathematics and reading is not only absurd, it is also extremely unfair to teachers.

When I was an elementary school principal with Chicago Public Schools (2007-2015), three online tests a year were imposed on children from Kindergarten through 8th grade (Test provider NWEA: North West Evaluation Association). As a result, a child from K through 8th grade was tested 27 times with NWEA and eight times for ISAT, a total of 35 times during elementary school! Needless to say, taking those tests reduces the amount of teaching time thus making it more difficult for teachers to attain yearly learning goals for all students.

As a comparison, elementary school students in France are tested only in 3rd and 6th grade and take extensive written exams in 9th and 12th grade (Baccalaureate). The main purpose of the 3rd and 6th grade tests is to evaluate if the national curriculum is effective, not to evaluate students, teachers, and schools because teachers do not control the level of poverty or the number of students with special needs.

In 2011, absurdity was paramount when Obama's Department of Education added the Early Learning Challenge that awarded schools showing that their students were ready to begin school. How? By having four-year-old children take "entry assessments". As educators know, this does not make any sense so why would the Department of Education do this then? Follow the money. Who benefits from more testing? Testing companies!

Pearson, the world's largest education (British) company, has the lion's share in the US testing market with more than

$9 billion of revenue annually. McGraw-Hill, Pearson's main competitor, gets over $2 billion in revenue and provides mostly the TerraNova and California Achievement Tests. Other testing providers include Education Testing Services, as well as Riverside Publishing and its parent company Houghton Mifflin Harcourt.

Corporations providing testing received hundreds of millions of public funding since the implementation of standardized testing.
Bob Schaeffer, public education director of FairTest, a nonprofit organization working to prevent the misuse of standardized testing, blames politicians, rather than corporations, for the testing boom. He said: "In a capitalist society, if there is a market, somebody will figure out how to serve it. But the corporations reinforce the stupidity of the bad policies of politicians."

To summarize, why do I think standardized testing is a disaster?

- It is an insult to multiple intelligences offering poor or even absurd content (Example: Pearson's passage about a race between a hare and a pineapple given to New-York 8th grade students)

- It gives the illusion that a narrow content is properly evaluated.

- It only tests mathematics and reading rote superficial learning

- It is not adapted to many students with special needs even with the accommodations provided.

- It increases the levels of stress for the vast majority of students and educators because it determines students' graduation and promotion as well as teachers' and administrators' evaluations.

- The tests are chocked full of errors.

- People conceiving and scoring the tests are not qualified.

- Political decisions on essential educational policies are influenced by profit motivated testing companies that finance political campaigns and have lobbyists in Washington pushing their agendas. For instance, Pearson played a critical role in creating the new Common Core Standards because they had an interest in designing and selling new tests to all 50 states.

- Research has shown that more testing does not reduce the gaps and did not improve the U.S. international ranking in math and reading.

**The perverse effects that over- testing has succeeded in producing are:**

- Focus on math and reading at the expense of all other subjects decreases the creativity of students.

- Cheating practices: scandals have been documented in at least 37 states. A superintendent in El Paso is currently serving jail time for cheating and forcing low-scoring students to drop out of school, a practice that many charters schools have adopted

- A lack of time for the development of social-emotional learning, as well as life skills

If you speak the truth about the absurdity of standardized testing, especially for special education students, you will be at risk of being fired like Sarah Chambers, a Chicago teacher who shared: "There's really an attack against me, because I'm an outspoken union activist, and especially an outspoken special education advocate. They cut special education by $80 million this year alone, and it's really hurting our students," she said. "I have spoken at the Board of Education, and brought parents and students to speak at the Board of Education, and frankly they want teachers to be silent. You know, they want them to follow their orders, and I can't be silent, because it hurts my students with disabilities."

http://chicago.cbslocal.com/2017/04/11/sarah-chambers-special-education-teacher-cps-firing-critic/

While politicians have forced ill-conceived, repetitive, money-making standardized tests down the throats of administrators, teachers and students, most politicians and policy makers have been enrolling their children in private schools that do not use standardized testing. Sandy Kress, one of the architects of President Bush's No Child Left Behind sent her son to a private Latin school. President Obama's daughters went to the exclusive $30,000/year Lab School of Chicago then at the $30,000/year Sidwell Friends School in Washington, D.C. The two most recent mayors of Chicago (Richard Daley and Rahm Emmanuel) sent their children to private schools. The current Secretary of Education Betsy Devos is a billionaire that has never been to public school herself nor has she enrolled her own children into public schools. Having no experience in education, she can pave the way for all private charter operators who cannot wait to get their hands on more taxpayer money. It is fundamentally flawed to think education is an area where companies should generate profits. Education is an investment in the youth of a country that should benefit both the students and the country. Students benefit from obtaining good paying jobs that will ensure a comfortable standard of living, while the country will see a return on investment in the form a highly skilled and well-educated work force that pays taxes.

# CHAPTER 6

# TEACHERS

Without nurses, hospitals would not be able to operate. Without teachers, schools cannot function unless for-profit companies soon come up with teaching robots! Who knows what private charter operators will bring!

Even though people often comment: "You are a teacher! That's wonderful, what a noble profession!", the same people do not encourage their own children to pursue this career. They know deep inside that these "noble" jobs are not valued in our present society and do not pay as well as well-respected professions such as lawyer, doctor, engineer, businessman, hedge fund manager or good-paying jobs such as electrician and plumber.

Bill McDiarmid who led the Carnegie-funded "Teachers for a New Era" project, points to the erosion of teaching's image as a stable career. There's a growing sense, he says, that K-12 teachers simply have less control over their professional lives in an increasingly bitter, politicized environment.

The main reasons teachers quit are the salary (teachers make on average 20% less than college graduates in other fields), lack of ability to voice their opinion, the working conditions, the obsession with standardized testing and the fact teaching is too often a thankless job.
http://www.npr.org/sections/ed/2016/10/24/495186021/what-are-the-main-reasons-teachers-call-it-quits

No wonder there is currently a crisis in teacher enrollment and America is also facing a serious teacher shortage! The enrollment of new teachers is down on average 35% and experienced teachers are no longer staying in their positions. Some states register grim numbers: in California, teacher enrollment fell about 50% over the past five years and New York and Texas have sharp decreases as well. Why is that? The reason is simple: why would young people decide to become teachers if they do not feel respected and supported? They know about the lack of resources and poor salaries not keeping up with the cost of living. They also have to consider their university cost and return on investment. With a cost of college that has been growing exponentially as we will see in Chapter 9, only high paying jobs will allow them to repay their student loans as rapidly as possible and still live comfortably.

Not only is there a crisis to recruit new teachers but experienced teachers are leaving or opting for early retirement.
They are discouraged by the unfair evaluation policies adopted in many states during the eight years of Obama.

They also cannot subscribe anymore to the over-testing of students that has no real educational value. As we have seen in Chapter 5, the intelligence of the youth should not be measured by math and reading standardized tests. The irony is that teachers who do not teach mathematics and reading are also evaluated on the mathematics and reading results of the students. In this system of excessive reliance on tests, children as well as teachers become the victims of inadequate policies.

According to the Organization for Economic Co-operation and Development, the United States ranks 4th in the number of hours required from teachers (after Columbia, Chile and Mexico) while it ranks 10th for compensation (far behind Luxembourg and Korea).
Sources:
(OECD:http://www.oecd-ilibrary.org/education/education-at-a-glance-2016/indicator-d4-how-much-time-do-teachers-spend-teaching_eag-2016-32-en )

http://www.huffingtonpost.com/tom-ostapchuk/most-and-least-paid-teachers-in-the-world_b_8970800.html

No wonder then that many teachers have been quitting at the rate of 8% a year in 2016, twice more than high-performing countries like Finland or Singapore. The teaching force is "a leaky bucket, losing hundreds of thousands of teachers each year — the majority of them before retirement age," says a recent report from the Learning Policy Institute.

**The following open letter written in 2016 by Steven Wedel, 2014 Teacher of the Year says it all. It is a heartbreaking testimony.**

## Open Letter to Oklahoma Voters and Lawmakers

I am a teacher. I teach English at the high-school of an independent district within Oklahoma City. I love my job. I love your kids. I call them my kids. I keep blankets in my room for when they're cold. I feed them peanut butter crackers, beef jerky, or Pop Tarts when Michelle Obama's school breakfast or lunch isn't enough to fill their bellies. I comfort them when they cry and I praise them when they do well and always I try to make them believe that they are somebody with unlimited potential no matter what they go home to when they leave me.

What do they go home to? Sometimes when they get sick at school they can't go home because you and the person you're currently shacking up with are too stoned to figure out it's your phone ringing. Sometimes they go home to parents who don't notice them, and those are often the lucky kids. Sometimes they go home to sleep on the neighbor's back porch because your boyfriend kicked them out of the house and his dog is too mean to let them sleep on their own back porch. They go home to physical and verbal abuse. They go home looking for love and acceptance from the people who created them ... and too often they don't find it.

Many days your children bring the resentment they feel toward you to school with them and they act out against peers, property, or their teachers. When I call you, I'm told, "When he's at school he's your problem." Or you beat them, not for what they did, but because it embarrassed or inconvenienced you when I called. Often, they stay at school with me for an hour and a half after the bell rings because they don't want to go home to you. Reluctantly, they get on the two buses meant to take home students who stay for athletic practice, and they go away for a dark night in places I can't imagine.

Over 90 percent of the kids in my high school are on the free or reduced lunch programs. The walk hand-in-hand with Poverty and its brother Violence. They find comfort in the arms of your lover, Addiction. They make babies before they are old enough to vote or drive. And they continue the cycle you put them in.

Sometimes I get through to a student and convince her that education is the way out of this spiral of poverty and despair. Then you slap them down for wanting to be better than you.

And you, the lawmakers of this state, you encourage it. I hold two college degrees and have been on my job for 10 years. I was our school's Teacher of the Year in 2014. I teach kids to read the ballots that keep you in your elite position. I teach them to look behind your lies and rhetoric. I teach them to think for themselves. The compensation of me and my colleagues ranks 49th in the nation, and is the lowest in our region. I currently earn about $18,000 per year less than I did in 2002, my last year as an office worker for an energy company that merged with another and eliminated my job. I feel like my life has purpose now, but, as I turn 50 this year and wonder how I'll put my own high school-age kids through college, I have to consider giving up helping scores of kids per year so I can afford to give my own children what they need to find satisfaction in their lives.

And what do you do? You whittle away at education funding. You waste the taxpayers' money so that our great state faces unbelievable shortfalls and massive budget cuts. You take home a salary that ranks 10th highest in the nation among state legislators and you are inept, uncaring, and an abomination to our democratic form of government.

Those kids who stay after school with me? After Spring Break 2016, they can't do that. You see, our district can no longer afford to pay to run those late buses. Your kids wade through garbage in the halls because we had to release the custodial crew that cleaned at night. Oh sure, we could make the kids clean up after themselves, except our administrators live in fear of lawsuits, and making a kid pick up the lunch tray he threw on the floor has been considered forced child labor. There's also the very real possibility that a belligerent kid will just take a swing at one of us — again — because he or she wasn't taught respect for authority at home.

Did I mention how we had to let go of our security officers because we could no longer afford them? We now share one single solitary Oklahoma County Sheriff's deputy with our ninth-grade center and our middle school and alternative school. That's one deputy for about 1,300 students.

We can no longer afford rolls of colored paper or paint or tape to make signs to support and advertise our Student Council activities. This fall our football team won't charge through a decorated banner as they take the field because we can't afford to make the banner. There won't be any new textbooks in the foreseeable future. Broken desks won't be replaced. We're about to ration copy paper and we've already had the desktop printers taken out of our rooms.

We live in fear that our colleagues will leave us, not just because they are our friends, but because the district wouldn't replace them even if we could lure new teachers to our inner-city schools during the teacher shortage you have caused. We fear our classes doubling in size.

We fear becoming as ineffective as you are. Not because we can't or won't do our job, like you, but because you keep passing mandates to make us better while taking away all the resources we need just to maintain the status quo. We fear that our second jobs will prevent us from grading the papers or creating the lesson plans we already have to do from home. We fear our families will leave us because we don't have time for them.

I am the chairman of my department. My teachers could easily take other jobs in the private sector where they would make more money, but so far, they have chosen to remain teachers because they love working with kids. How long will they continue to put the needs of students over the needs of family? It's something we're all dealing with. How far will you push us? What will you do without us when we leave the classroom or leave the state? It's happening. You know it's happening, and yet you do nothing.

You, the representatives, senators, and governor of Oklahoma are creating a population of ignorant peasants fit only to work in the oil field and factories you bring to this state by promising those businesses won't have to pay their fair share of taxes. You leave our kids in a cycle of poverty and abuse while your pet donor oil companies destroy the bedrock beneath us, shaking our homes to pieces while you deny your part in all of it.

Parents, I beg you to love your children the way we love your children. Vote for people who will help teachers educate and nurture the kids we share. We can't do it alone anymore.

**Source:** https://stevenewedel.wordpress.com/2016/02/26/open-letter-to-oklahoma-voters-and-lawmakers/

# CHAPTER 7

# THE PRIVATIZATION OF EDUCATION

Privatization of the public sector means privately run organizations use taxpayer funding. The most familiar U.S. example is the privatization of federal prisons that occurred in the 1980s. Public schools are one of the latest bastions that private companies have not yet completely taken over. Lobbyists have been successful since 2000 in convincing politicians to not only reward private companies with huge contracts related to education (testing, technology, textbooks, food, maintenance, cleaning services, etc.) but also to accelerate the closing of public schools and shift the funding to more charter and private schools.

Districts and states that have huge deficits seem to find it interesting to transfer their responsibility to educate the youth. They replace traditional public schools with charter schools managed by non-profit organizations and for-profit contractors. The erroneous assumption is that they will succeed where public schools have failed. They operate as autonomous public schools through waivers from many of the requirements mandated by state and districts for traditional public schools. In many cases, they achieve better results because they are not bound by the same rules. For instance, they can select their students as they wish while neighborhood public schools must enroll all students living in the assigned attendance area. Having the possibility to select students equates to a form of discrimination which certainly gives charters an unfair advantage.

Milton Friedman was the first to introduce the idea of school privatization as early as 1955. He wrote "The Role of Government in Education", an essay proposing that government provide parents with voucher to pay for free-market education. In 1996, Milton Friedman created the Friedman Foundation for Educational Choice (later renamed EdChoice) as "the nation's only organization solely dedicated to promoting educational choice." His advocacy for vouchers, charter schools, and tax credits for private school tuition has contributed to the siphoning of tax dollars out of the public-school system into charter and corporate operations.

In 1994, the Clinton administration created the federal Charter Schools Program (CSP). Did Clinton embrace market-based education reform as he embraced privatizations of prisons because he needed campaign funding from corporate America? It would not be surprising. The Charter Schools Program has been giving three-year grants to states on a competitive basis for the purpose of opening or expanding charter schools.

In school year 2016/17, there were approximately 3 million students attending 6,900 charter schools, six times more than in 2000. The closing of public schools has been simultaneous. In 2015, 270 schools were closed for low enrollment, lack of funding or poor performance while more than 400 charters schools opened. Minnesota was the first state to pass a charter school law in 1991. California was second, in 1992. In 2015, as many as 43 states and the District of Columbia had charter school laws, according to the Center for Education Reform. Washington D.C. corporate lobbyists have been busy and productive!

"School choice" is the genius idea to promote publicly funded charter schools. Why would parents oppose such a concept? They are sold on it and do not realize that "public good" has true value. They are brainwashed and do not know that charters are financed by taxpayers' dollars. "All parents should be able to choose the school that's best for their children" is a statement that wins parent approval, the same way "No Child Left Behind" or "College and Career Ready" succeeded in winning parent support to test their children ad nauseam.

Having taxpayers pick up the tab for parents' private choice is a flawed and unfair way to reform education because it will mostly benefit the upper class. Advocates of a free-market education system cannot ignore that this system will create even more inequality because middle and upper class parents will be able to pay for the top private schools while the lower-middle class and poor will not be able to afford the schools with the highest demand. So, they will enroll their children in "government" schools, in other words, the "left-overs".

As the corporate approach is winning politician's support over the community-based education reform, we are going to witness in the coming years even more public resources shifted away from public schools in order to subsidize the country's private and religious schools with vouchers. This shift will evidently deplete as a result the already inadequate resources allocated to neighborhood public schools. (See following pages: tables comparing and contrasting two approaches of Education Reform).

Another underlying political goal of the privatization of public schools is of course to marginalize Teacher Unions as many charter, private and religious schools do not allow teachers to unionize. Therefore, merchants can dictate questionable educational methods while silencing the teachers hired to implement them.

The principle of schools as public good is no longer considered or even discussed. The reality is that all public schools should be places where diverse children learn to live together and respect each other. When I was principal at LaSalle Language Academy, I have experienced first-hand that a racially and socio economically diverse school by design works well for all students, as proven by the Blue Ribbon award received in 2015. This kind of school bridges the gaps between different races and socio economic status. Unfortunately, too many public schools are still not diverse as they welcome a population of students that only reflects the value of real estate in the area.

# Comparison of two reform approaches

Source: http://strongerschools.blogspot.com/2013/03/education-reform-corporate-vs-community.html

| Corporate-based reform | Issue | Community-based reform |
|---|---|---|
| **Teachers and schools are to blame**<br><br>Differently managed schools can overcome any and all of the negative effects of poverty. Our schools are failing because of bad teachers and bad schools. Fix them and we will fix our test scores and fix our society. | **Problem Statement** | **Poverty is the problem**<br>US school outcomes from the top-tiers are outstanding. The problem lies in the lower quartile where there is rampant *child poverty* and its negative effects. Children who come to school hungry, abused, come from broken homes, from parents who care little about education will almost never succeed no matter how great the teacher or the school. |

| Schools should be like corporations | Solution Summary | Fight poverty |
|---|---|---|
| They should be *privately* run, and run by the numbers. We should find the best teachers who will work for the lowest pay and job security. Children must be tested more, and test scores should be the primary driver for *everything*, especially for firing teachers and closing schools. Citizens should be able to choose schools like they choose any other product from a corporation. | | Our lowest-scoring areas need **community programs** that give children the same kinds of benefits that higher-scoring students have, such as stable health care, early education, stable and caring adult role models, and a consistent focus on education. The profession of teaching should be *elevated* not denigrate. |

| **Parents choose** | **Segregation** | **Separate is unequal** |
|---|---|---|
| If parents wish to segregate themselves using taxpayer dollars, that's their "choice". If they wish to excuse themselves and their family from the downsides of the system they themselves voted to burden with extra responsibilities, they may. Schools should no more be a central part of a community than a convenience store or a gas station. | | Segregation in any form is wrong, and contrary to Brown v. Board of Education. School and/or program selection should be done using democratically agreed-upon objective factors, including practical factors like geography and school facilities, and individual factors such as a child's special needs. Everyone follows the same rules and everybody works together to improve their local neighborhood school, which is the permanent heart of the community. |

| Privatization and profits | Governance | Democracy |
|---|---|---|
| Schools should be privately run and parents should be "consumers" who shop around for schools like they shop for car insurance or a bank. If a local school fails, parents simply move on to the next one. Parents care only about themselves and their own children. K-12 education in the USA is a "trillion dollar opportunity" and we should allow a new form of "entrepreneurs" to chase after every cent of it. | | Schools should be public and take all comers, and they should be pillars of the community. Everybody works together for the betterment of the community school and come together there. Parents work to better their school as they work to better their community. The profit motive does not belong in *public* education and serves only to provide a corrupting influence--it creates an "education-industrial complex" which is dangerous to democracy. |

| High-stakes testing | Accounta-bility | Contextual management |
|---|---|---|
| Teachers are not professionals and they shouldn't be treated that way. Accountability is achieved through testing. Teachers whose tests scores fall are fired. Failing schools are closed and replaced by charter schools. Testing should be done extensively, and often. It should only test the basics and ignore subjects like history and literature. | | Teachers should be managed like the *professionals* they are. Real management is contextual, and involves judgment. Some teachers may have harder assignments and mitigating factors. Testing should be used only as the blunt diagnostic tool it is, and emphasis should be placed on overall quality as decided upon by community standards, parents and other professionals. |

| "Choice" | Equality | Objective equality |
|---|---|---|
| Parents decide on schools for whatever reason they choose, regardless of motivations. Parents should be able to segregate themselves however they like. All students should receive exactly the same amount of funding regardless of need. | | Democratically decided rules and practical factors (such as geography) determine the placement of students in schools, which are all part of the same system and take all comers. Democratically-controlled schools establish objective rules for special programs. Funding should be prioritized according to student needs. |

Source: http://strongerschools.blogspot.com/2013/03/education-reform-corporate-vs-community.html

# CHAPTER 8

# SCHOOL CURRICULA

Another surprise I had when I studied the American education system was the national mess regarding the U.S. school curricula. Coming from France where there is a rigorous national curriculum and teachers are trained to implement the very same curriculum in all regions, I was questioning why the U.S., in the 21st century, still did not come up with common curricula and common evaluation for its youth across states.

This common reference for content provides a reliable profile of students' competencies when they move from one region to the other.
I found out that each U.S. state and even each district within the same state could determine the content of student learning. This freedom would be commend-

able if there were not so many variables associated with an infinite amount of curricula such as:

- Difficulty to compare students' mastery levels across states and across districts within a state
- Difficulty and waste of time for teachers to adapt when moving from one district to the other or one state to another
- Incoherence of content offered in textbooks within the same state
- District level of resources impacting curriculum development
- Reliance on state evaluation systems to create curricula
- Dependence on Board of Education members' belief systems, which can be dangerous going as far as rejecting science knowledge that contradicts religious beliefs
- A waste of resources because each district has to reinvent the wheel

# The Failure of the Common Core Standards

State governors, convinced that some uniformity was necessary initiated the now infamous Common Core Standards initiative in 2009. It was a laudable initiative.

According to the common core standards official website: "The state-led effort to develop the Common Core State Standards was launched in 2009 by state leaders, including governors and state commissioners of education from 48 states, two territories and the District of Columbia, through their membership in the National Governors Association Center for Best Practices (NGA Center) and the Council of Chief State School Officers (CCSSO). State school chiefs and governors recognized the value of consistent, real-world learning goals and launched this effort to ensure all students, regardless of where they live, are graduating high school prepared for college, career, and life."

http://www.corestandards.org/about-the-standards/development-process/

## The PARCC Failure

The main reason the Common Core Standards and the Partnership for Assessment of Readiness for College and Careers (PARCC) failed was because it was based on the flawed assumption that evaluation drives curricula. On the contrary, curricula drives evaluation. Who would blame teachers for adapting their teaching and curriculum to what they and their students are going to be evaluated on? Instead of creating coherent and rigorous curricula from early childhood to high school, the Common Core Standards only defined goals to achieve in each grade.

It's as if they wanted all children to reach the top of Everest by 18 years old but teachers were given no indication as to how to achieve that goal. They could only see for each year of schooling marks 1 to 12, and were given the impossible task of embarking all students to the summit including those who do not understand English, those who are hearing-impaired or blind, those who are missing a leg, those whose cognitive impairments prevent them from understanding what you are saying.

The Common Core Standards initiative did not create curricula. It created arbitrary benchmarks to be reached and strictly measured with standardized tests without taking into account the diversity of students, including English learners and students with special needs.

Soon after the Common Core Standards initiative was launched, the associated tool to evaluate students pompously called Partnership for Assessment of

Readiness for College and Careers (PARCC) was created by the private company Pearson Inc. It was another fancy name aimed at convincing parents that each child would complete high school "College and Career ready".

Encouraged by the U.S. Department of Education "Race to the Top" grants, in 2010, the District of Columbia and 24 states had adopted PARCC: Alabama, Arizona, Arkansas, Colorado, Delaware, Florida, Georgia, Illinois, Indiana, Kentucky, Louisiana, Maryland, Massachusetts, Mississippi, New Jersey, New Mexico, New York, North Dakota, Ohio, Oklahoma, Pennsylvania, Rhode Island, and Tennessee.

Progressively, states withdrew, first Florida in 2013, citing unconstitutional involvement by the federal government in states' affairs, then by 2014, Alabama, Delaware, Florida, Georgia, Indiana, Kentucky, North Dakota, Pennsylvania, Tennessee, and Utah. This was following increasing concerns about the Common Core Standards and a high cost of testing estimated in July 2013 at $29.50 per-student, almost $3 million for a state having to evaluate 100,000 students!

As of July 2016, only nine active PARCC members were remaining: Colorado, the District of Columbia, Illinois, Louisiana, Maryland, Massachusetts, New Jersey, New Mexico, and Rhode Island.

Many financially challenged states had adopted the initiative because Obama's Secretary of Education Arne Duncan had attached substantial federal grants as a carrot on a stick. It gave the illusion that the initiative was a success when in fact, it was a complete failure.

# CHAPTER 9

# THE OUTRAGEOUS COST OF HIGHER EDUCATION

If your child does not excel in a special talent or does not qualify for merit-based college scholarships, you are out of luck. In 2017, graduates who borrow to pay for college are leaving school with an average of $34,000 in student loans. That's up from $20,000 just 10 years ago, according to a new analysis from the Federal Reserve Bank of New York.

https://www.newyorkfed.org/press/pressbriefings/household-borrowing-student-loans-homeownership

In addition, there is a high probability that they will not be able to find a good paying job for several years, forcing them to delay the re-payment of their loan, generating an added cost.

**Be prepared to pay from $3,520 to over $55,000 a year!** According to 2016 data from the College Board, you will have to pay on average per year in tuition:

| | |
|---|---|
| $3,520 | for a public two-year college |
| $9,650 | for a public four-year college if the college is in your state of residence |
| $24,930 | for a public four-year college that is not in your state of residence |
| $33,480 | for a private non-profit four-year college |

Add food, lodging and supplies and you are looking at a minimum of $12,000 a year and up to $50,000 a year.

## What About Ivy League Colleges?

The yearly attendance and tuition fees for 2016/17 were the following:

| Universities | Attendance Fees |
|---|---|
| Columbia | $55,056 |
| Pennsylvania | $51,464 |
| Dartmouth | $51,438 |
| Brown | $51,366 |
| Cornell | $50,953 |
| Yale | $49,480 |
| Harvard | $47,074 |
| Princeton | $45,320 |

Add food, lodging and supplies and you are now looking at $75,000 a year on average for Ivy League Universities. How can a family making $20,000 a year afford to send their children to these universities? The answer is simple: they cannot. American parents and students are used to these costs and resort to borrowing, which is of course great for the finance industry.

**In France, college tuition fees are between $200 and $650 a year!**
The tuition for French public universities for 2016/17 was:
184 Euros/year    Two-year Bachelor
256 Euros/year    Master
391 Euros/year    Doctorate degree
610 Euros/year    Engineer degree

Source:http://www.enseignementsup-recherche.gouv.fr/cid20195/frais-d-inscription-pour-la-rentree-universitaire-2016.html

Many social-democracies in Europe (Sweden, Finland, Netherlands, etc.) have similar low costs or none, and even sometimes pay students a stipend during their studies. After I passed the selective exam (1/10 ratio) to enter the "Ecole Normale d'Instituteurs" in Paris in 1985, I was paid minimum wage (around $1,200 a month in 1985) to become a national certified teacher with a promise to teach at least 10 years in exchange for the salary received for two years.

University tuition levels say a lot about the priorities of a country: profit or investment? What a difference between France and the U.S.!

There is a detail often forgotten in the USA where wars have been too often used to stimulate, sustain the economy or sometimes sadly help a president raise his popularity ratings: ESEA (**Elementary and Secondary Education Act)** allows military recruiters access

11th and 12th grade students' information. This is not surprising since the U.S. is first and foremost a War Nation, with half of its budget devoted to its "Defense Budget" (or should we say "Attack Budget"?). A War Nation needs soldiers and if the youth cannot afford university, they will more easily be tempted to enroll in the armed services to receive training at no cost, except possibly the risk to die while deployed.

Bernie Sanders, U.S. Senator for Vermont and 2016 presidential candidate is one of the few politicians fighting to pass new legislation to reduce the cost of college. He said in April 2017:

"There are millions of hardworking students in this country who deserve better than to be tens of thousands of dollars in debt, to be unable to buy a house or to start a family just because they wanted to get an education. It really is ridiculous that as a nation we are discouraging people from getting an education because of the cost of college. That is crazy! But it does not have to be this way. Countries around the world have made college tuition-free, and so can the United States. I recently introduced legislation to do that and make public colleges and universities tuition-free for working families. We can have the most educated workforce in the world. We just have to think bigger than we are now, and stop punishing people for seeking education."

"Young people in this country are not going to succeed unless we have the best educated workforce in the world. That means making public colleges and universities tuition-free—not making it so expensive that people are literally going hungry to get an education."

# CHAPTER 10

# TRAPPING CITIZENS FOR LIFE VIA STUDENT DEBT

Who benefits the most from the outrageous cost of higher education? Private colleges and lenders! Who do they trap the most? Certainly, not the millionaires and billionaires who do not need to borrow to pay for their children's education. They do trap the low and medium income parents or their children, ideal preys as they rightfully want degrees to increase their chance to a higher salary.

The increasing cost of higher education created a profitable loan market. As of April 2017, Americans owe over $1.41 trillion in student loan debt and there are 44.2 million borrowers. That is $620 billion more than the total U.S. credit card debt which is also staggering! The average Class of 2016 graduate has

$37,172 in student loan debt, up six percent from 2015.

About 40 percent of the $1.4 trillion student loan debt was used to finance graduate and professional degrees. The combined average undergraduate and graduate debt by degree per student is:

| | |
|---|---|
| MBA | $42,000 |
| Master of Education | $50,879 |
| Master of Science | $50,400 |
| Master of Arts | $58,539 |
| Law | $140,616 |
| Medecine-Health-Sciences | $161,772 |

As debt statistics show, the cost of attending college is becoming a growing burden for a large portion of Americans.

Not surprisingly, the student loan delinquency rate is high at 11.2% (90+ days delinquent or in default). The average student loan payment for borrower aged 20 to 30 years is $351 a month.
Source (2016)
https://studentloanhero.com/student-loan-debt-statistics/

The U.S. Department of Education contracts with four main lenders: American Education Services-Pennsylvania Higher Education Loan Program (AES-PHEAA), Great Lakes, Neinet, and Navient. Their websites are communicating how easy it is to borrow and the flexibility students have to repay the loans. Students have a "grace period" explained as follows on the Great Lakes website:

"After you leave school or drop below half-time enrollment, you enter your grace period, a six-month period of time before you are required to make payments on your student loans. Even though it's not required, making payments during this time can reduce the amount of interest that is capitalized or prevent interest from capitalizing."

Then for repayment, the lender explains: "Federal loans have a variety of repayment plans, ranging from 10 years to 30 years, and some plans offer flexible repayment terms that look at your income and family size to determine your monthly payment. Federal loans are unique because they offer more options for postponing payments than other loans do, including deferment and forbearance."

Currently, there is a lawsuit against Navient, one of the largest student loans lenders. As reported by Forbes, "Navient, is last among major lenders in enrolling borrowers in affordable student loan repayment plans such as PAYE (Pay As You Earn) and REPAYE (Revised Pay As You Earn). Could Navient's low sign-up rate for student loan repayment plans have led to more borrower defaults? This is what the lawsuit is about…

When students default, they can refinance their debt with other lenders such as SoFi, DRB, CommonBond, LendKey, Citizens Bank, College Ave, all charging on average interests between 3% and 8%.

Those who cannot refinance are defaulting says Rohit Chopra, at the Consumer Federation of America:
"3,000 preventable student loan defaults each day in America is 3,000 too many. **Our broken system works well for the student loan industry, but is failing borrowers, taxpayers and our economy."**

Source: https://www.forbes.com/sites/zack-friedman/2017/03/17/student-loans-navient-defaults/#34e0297c684d

It's all good, right? The growth of the US economy has been based on credit for many years. That's how the system works. The government uses bonds to finance the long costly wars. Consequence? At the end of 2017 the gross U.S. federal government debt is estimated at $20.1 trillion, according to the FY18 Federal Budget posted on usgovernmentdebt.us

States and cities overuse bonds to finance their operations, sometimes reaching junk bond ratings after having sold assets to private interests, such as the parking system or the Skyway in Chicago.

Young Americans receive 0% credit card offers early on and get sucked into a debt cycle they were not educated to handle. Meanwhile, banks charge 18% interest to those who cannot pay the credit card balance on time because usually, the attractive 0% rate no longer applies after 6 or 12 months.

Why would politicians decide to shift more money from the defense budget to subsidize higher education and reduce college costs? After all, banks and lenders help pay for their campaigns! The problem is that citizens get trapped with compounded interest and often remain in debt for most of their lives.

**According to a 2016 GOBankingRates survey, 69% of Americans have less than $1,000 in their savings accounts and about half of US families have zero retirement account savings.** Without savings, more and more have to keep working well after 65.

Source: http://www.cnbc.com/2016/10/03/how-much-americans-at-every-age-have-in-their-savings-accounts.html

During President Obama's eight years in office, 8.7 million Americans defaulted on their student loans (one default every 29 seconds!). Doesn't this prove that the system set to help students is flawed? How can young professionals succeed in life if they start off with debt that prevents them from living decently? No wonder many have to live with their parents past 25 years old because they can simply not afford to be financially independent. Student debt often prevents young professionals from buying a home. How can they save for a downpayment and borrow when they can barely repay their student debt? Owning a home used to be the main indicator of middle class success in America, but not anymore.

Finally, aware of this serious issue, President Obama issued in 2016 memorandums to require that the government's Federal Student Aid office (spending annually around $800 million to collect on $1.4 trillion of government-owned student loans debt.), do more to help borrowers manage, or even discharge, their debt. In 2017, in a memorandum to the Department's Student Aid office, Trump's Secretary of Education DeVos withdrew the Obama memos. Borrowers are no longer protected. This shows clearly that the Trump administration cares more for the success of loan contractors than for students' welfare.

Isn't the vicious circle of debt a wonderful opportunity for the finance industry to keep increasing their profits at the expense of low and middle class citizens?

# CHAPTER 11

# MISSING OUT ON HUMAN & ECONOMIC POTENTIAL

All the previous chapters show the main flaws of the U.S. education system. In this chapter, we will try to estimate the damaging consequences: how much human potential and economic growth are lost by not having systems in place that favor affordable higher education access for all?

## Low Achievement Results and Alarming Gaps

Among the 34 democratic countries in the Organization for Economic Cooperation and Development (OECD), the United States ranks around 20th annually, receiving average or below-average grades in reading, science, and mathematics.

According to Harvard economist Roland G. Fryer Jr., **by 8th grade, only 44 percent of American students are proficient in reading and math.** The proficiency of African-American students, many of them attending underperforming schools, is even lower. "The position of U.S. black students is truly alarming," wrote Fryer, the Henry Lee Professor of Economics, who used the OECD rankings to come to this conclusion: "If they were to be considered a country, they would rank just below Mexico in last place."

"The gap between white and minority students has proven stubbornly difficult to close", says Ronald Ferguson, adjunct lecturer in public policy at Harvard Kennedy School and faculty director of Harvard's Achievement Gap Initiative. That gap extends along class lines as well. This is not a surprise, because very little has been done to address the gaps that occur during early childhood years when it matters most. This time is crucial because of its impact on the development of a child's brain and one's ability to learn other languages.

## Waste of Economic Wealth

In the fall of 2016, about 20.5 million students were expected to attend American colleges and universities immediately after finishing high school according to the U.S. Department of Education National Center of Education Statistics (NCES).
Source:
https://nces.ed.gov/programs/digest/d15/tables/dt15_105.20.asp?current=yes

In 2014, 30 million 18-24 year-old students were enrolled in degree-granting institutions.

Students enrolled in degree-granting institutions by race in 2014 (in %):

| Asian | 65.2% |
|---|---|
| Caucasian | 42.2% |
| Pacific Islander | 41% |
| Hispanic | 34.7% |
| African American | 32,6% |

What can we deduce from these numbers? The percentages of 18-24 year-olds NOT enrolled in any post high-school degree-granting program are alarmingly high.

Students NOT enrolled in degree-granting institutions in 2014 (in %)

| African American | 67.4% |
|---|---|
| Hispanic | 65.3% |
| Pacific Islander | 59% |
| Caucasian | 57.8% |
| Asian | 34.8% |

Considering that in 2015, adults with bachelor's degrees took home more than those with high school diplomas, we can calculate the economic impact of Americans not earning higher education degrees. Degree holders earned $48,500 a year on average, while high school diploma holders earned $23,900. Difference: $24,600 a year.

If we just imagine that 80% of all youth 18-24 year-old were pursuing at least a bachelor degree, there would be a large influx of higher salaries in the U.S. economy. That's about 10 million more individuals (a 1/3 of all 30 million) who would make $25,000 a year more once they graduate! That's $250 billion a year!

Over the last 20 years, imagine that a third more of the 24-44 year-old age group (82 million individuals) also had earned at minimum a bachelor degree. That would be 27 million more individ-

uals making $25,000 more per year, for a total of $675 billion a year!
Source: Census Bureau data (2010)

For these two groups, we would be looking at almost a trillion dollars more in salaries per year. Who would continue to argue that education is not a great investment to help grow the economy and lift people so they can at least reach middle class revenue levels?

# CHAPTER 12

# STEPS TOWARDS RADICAL CHANGE

**Step 1**
***Amend the U.S. Constitution and ALL State Constitutions*** to recognize Education as a Fundamental Right.

**Step 2**
***Ratify the Universal Declaration of Children Rights.***
This would show to the world that the wealthiest country on earth does care for its youth.

**Step 3**
***Reform the education funding system.***
How? Either increase the sales taxes or impose a uniform 10% tax for all E-Commerce transactions to finance education equally. Each state could collect

the sales taxes and allocate the funds per district according to the needs of their students. This would end the practice of bringing education to the lowest denominator depending too often on minimum and insufficient resources. This would also eliminate the disparities between rich and poor districts.

Another benefit would be to allocate the real estate tax to other purposes such as hiring social workers to work in poor neighborhoods and invest to re-gentrify these areas.

In one of its decisions, the Supreme Court characterized the Texas school system as "chaotic and unjust" and emphasized the need for reform in a tax system that "relied too long and too heavily on the local property tax." Unfortunately, the severe opinion of the Court does not carry the power to change the U.S. education funding system.

**Step 4**
***Adopt national elementary and high school curricula.***
There are many districts and excellent schools in the country that came up with rigorous curricula and teaching methods adapted to the 21st century. Why re-invent the wheel? Share the wealth!

**Step 5**
***Build public preschools.***
In 2009, I was very disappointed that the Obama administration did not start investing in preschools instead of allocating millions to the meaningless "Race to the Top" that resulted in more testing and more privatization of public schools. No wonder the U.S. is not bridging the gaps between rich and poor or between students from different racial backgrounds! Public education should start well before 5 years old as explained in Chapter 2. France opens its early childhood public schools as early as 2 and a half years old if the child is toilet trained.

This greatly helps in developing many skills, detecting impairments early, and accelerating the integration of children of immigrants.

## Step 6
***Value and Expand Vocational Community Colleges.***
Vocational schools are two-year colleges which prepare students to enter the workforce after they receive an Associate degree.

## Step 7
***Address poverty with financial aid and more social workers.***
There is a vicious circle of poverty when education is not lifting the youth. Addressing poverty starts with recognizing that there is a problem and offering higher education financial aid to low-income families as well as social workers and counselors to help navigate higher education options. In 2015, Public Broadcasting Service (PBS) reported

that "the National Center for Children in Poverty found that 44 percent of the nation's children live in low-income households, according to 2013 data from the U.S. Census Bureau's 2013 American Community Survey. The Great Recession may be over, but the number of children living in poverty or low-income families is still higher than pre-recession levels."
http://www.pbs.org/newshour/rundown/nccp-finds-44-percent-u-s-children-live-low-income-families/

## Step 8
***Recognize the true value of the work of teachers.***
What is more important in a country than preparing the youth to become a productive member of society? In order to achieve this goal, teachers must be highly selected and trained to become exceptional professionals. They also need support during their career and time to prepare and discuss the best les-

son plans with their colleagues. In China, teachers are working in classrooms half time and collaborating with their colleagues the other half time.

Talented students will not embrace the teaching profession if the highest respect is not shown with quality training and more than decent salaries. If this does not change, young professionals will rather study law, business, computer science or engineering.

Note: Refer to the letter written by the English high school teacher in Chapter 6 "I currently earn about $18,000 per year less - as a teacher - than I did in 2002, my last year as an office worker for an energy company".

## Step 9
***Change the way schools operate: replace the 19th century "productive" model with current successful creative models.***

We already know that many structured jobs in the economy have disappeared and will continue disappearing. However, current graduates are still mostly trained to follow instructions, jump through meaningless hoops and succeed on standardized tests. They are at high risk of being marginalized and unemployed.

Children are born inquisitive, not afraid of taking risks, creative, and capable of learning from their mistakes. If schools would only focus on preserving these qualities, young adults would thrive more and be ready to adapt quickly to the job market changes.

## Step 10
***Adopt federal budgets that show a true commitment to education.***

As 2016 presidential candidate Bernie Sanders expressed in 2017:

"We spend more on defense than the next 12 nations combined. While millions of Americans lack decent housing, education and health care, President Trump wants to expand military spending by tens of billions of dollars, including $30 billion this year alone. Meanwhile, defense contractors become richer and richer as more than a third of spending on developing defense programs has been wasted on cost overruns. We do not need to add more to an already bloated defense budget. We need to take care of our people."

**In 2016, the Education Budget was 2% of a $4.1 Trillion Total Spending Budget, about $79 Billion, compared to 16% for Defense.**

Source: https://www.nationalpriorities.org/analysis/2015/presidents-2016-budget-in-pictures/presidents-proposed-total-spending-fy2016/

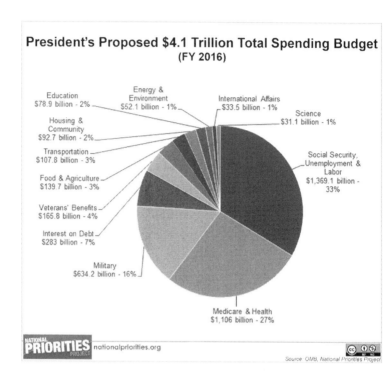

## Step 11
### *Reverse the 2010 five to four decision of the Supreme Court in Citizen United V. Federal Election Commission.*

The 2010 Supreme Court decision has allowed unlimited money in politics and is undermining the principles of democracy. As long as billionaires who have an interest in keeping low salaries will be able to buy politicians, there will be little chances to see the U.S. implement measures that would truly invest in its youth.

Former President Carter said that the Citizen United decision "violates the essence of what made America a great country and its political system. Now it's an oligarchy with unlimited political bribery being the essence of getting the nomination for president or elected president, the same thing applies to governors, U.S. Senators and Congress members. Now we have seen a complete subversion of our political system as a payoff to major contributors who expect and get favors for them after the election is over."

Occupied Democrats echoed Jimmy Carter's comments in stating: "Our proud republic has fallen into the grasping clutches of David and Charles Koch, Sheldon Adelson, Norman Braman,

Harold Simmons, Bob Perry, Joe Ricketts, Peter Thiel, Jerrold Perrenchio, Robert Mercer, Paul Singer, and all the other billionaires throwing their money around, buying themselves candidates and Congressmen."

# EPILOGUE

# CALL TO ACTION

The recently published 2017 Education budget proposed by the Trump administration unfortunately does not demonstrate that there is a will to progress in American education reforms towards social justice as shown in the document below:

## TRUMP'S BUDGET SLASHES EDUCATION

**90,000 KIDS**
KICKED OFF HEAD START EARLY EDUCATION

**1.1 MILLION KIDS**
KICKED OUT OF AFTER SCHOOL PROGRAMS

**1.5 MILLION STUDENTS**
LOSE COLLEGE GRANTS

**6 MILLION COLLEGE STUDENTS**
LOSE SUBSIDIZED LOANS

**330,000 STUDENTS**
LOSE WORK-STUDY

**PUBLIC SERVICE LOAN FORGIVENESS** ELIMINATED

BERNIE SANDERS

Even though France and United States initiated their Revolutions almost simultaneously and influenced each other's revolutionary principles and Constitutions, the United States Republic has developed as a very individualistic society based first and foremost on the value of freedom. In the meantime, France's motto "Liberté, Egalité, Fraternité" has resulted in more efforts towards equality of chances for all and fraternity. The contrast between France and U.S. education systems proves it. In the U.S., the political organization highly influenced by powerful lobbyists has undermined the chances to see changes in the way education of the American youth is valued.

Are there nevertheless reasons to be optimistic regarding possible changes in the way education is approached in the U.S.? Initiatives here and there seem to give some hope. For example, New-York state passing in 2017 a universal

public college tuition coverage that should help reduce student debt.
Source: http://www.nbcnews.com/news/education/new-york-becomes-first-state-offer-free-four-year-college-n744561

In Tennessee, a program called ACHIEVES is aspiring to provide scholarships to every needy high school graduate who wishes to attend one of the state's 13 community colleges or 27 technology centers.

In Atlanta, the East Lake neighborhood has turned a crime-laden slum with the city's lowest performing school into a prosperous neighborhood with one of the highest-performing schools in the state.

Philanthropists, such as Bill and Melinda Gates, are helping to send low-income students to college.

Despite the poor academic performance of students in many U.S. school districts, some states have shown that strong results are possible. For instance, if Massachusetts were a nation, it would rate among the best-performing countries (49% of college educated).
Source:
https://www.usnews.com/news/best-states/rankings/education

Let's hope that Congress and Senate will in a near future address the many flaws listed in this book. The elected representatives should read what President Kennedy recommended to Congress the year of his assassination.

**"Education is the keystone in the arch of freedom and progress.** Nothing has contributed more to the enlargement of this nation's strength and opportunities than our traditional system of free, universal elementary and secondary education, coupled with widespread availability of college education."

"A free Nation can rise no higher than the standard of excellence set in its schools and colleges. Ignorance and illiteracy, unskilled workers and school dropouts-these and other failures of our educational system breed failures in our social and economic system: delinquency, unemployment, chronic dependence, a waste of human resources, a loss of productive power and purchasing power and an increase in tax-supported benefits. **The loss of only one year's income due to unemployment is more than the total cost of twelve years of education through high school.** Failure to improve educational performance is thus not only poor social policy, it is poor economics."

Unfortunately, despite an increase in the percentage of students enrolled in post high school degrees since 1963, there are still too many young Americans who cannot afford to go to college. What will it take for the United States to step up its education game?

# AFTERWORD

Over 50 years ago, John Fitzgerald Kennedy, 35th President of the United States, delivered a long message to the Congress. He articulated all that needed to be done to give education the essential place it deserves.

Full speech at:
http://www.presidency.ucsb.edu/ws/?pid=9487

## Speech Highlights

**"For the nation, increasing the quality and availability of education is vital to both our national security and our domestic well being."**

**"In short, from every point of view, education is of paramount concern to the national interest as well as to each individual."**

"We can no longer afford the luxury of endless debate over all the complicated and sensitive questions raised by each new proposal on Federal participation in education."

"First, we must improve the quality of instruction provided in all of our schools and colleges. This requires more and better teachers--teachers who can be attracted to and retained in schools and colleges only if pay levels reflect more adequately the value of the services they render."

"Federal aid to college students is not new. More than 3 million World War II and Korean conflict veterans have received $6 billion in Federal funds since 1944 to assist them to attend college."

"A serious barrier to increased graduate study is the lack of adequate financial aid for graduate students."

"The welfare and security of the Nation require that we increase our investment in financial assistance for college students both at undergraduate and graduate levels."

"Improved research and teacher training are not enough, if good teachers do not choose to teach. Without sufficient incentive to make teaching a lifetime career, teachers with valuable training and experience but heavy family responsibilities too often become frustrated and drop out of the profession."

"Despite our high level of educational opportunity and attainment, nearly 23 million adult Americans lack an eighth grade education. They represent a staggering economic and cultural loss to their families and the Nation. I recommend again, as part of this comprehensive bill, a program to assist all States in offering literacy and basic education courses to adults."

"The program here proposed is reasonable and yet far-reaching. It offers Federal assistance without Federal control. It provides for economic growth, manpower development and progress toward our educational and humanitarian objectives."

JOHN F. KENNEDY

http://www.presidency.ucsb.edu/ws/?pid=9487

Made in the USA
Middletown, DE
19 April 2022